A Treatise Upon The Useful Science Of Defence

A

TREATISE

Upon the Ufeful

Science of Defence,

Connecting the

-SMALL and BACK-SWORD,

And fhewing th[e]   [ident]ity between them.

LIK[EWI]SE

Endeavouring to wee[d out] [par]t of thofe fuperfluous,
unmeaning Practices which over-run it, and choke
the true Principles, by reducing it to a narrow
Compafs, and fupporting it with Mathematical
Proofs.

ALSO

An Examination into the Performances of the moft Noted
MASTERS of the BACK-SWORD, who have fought upon
the Stage, pointing out their Faults, and allowing their
Abilities.

WITH

Some Obfervations upon BOXING, and the CHARACTERS of the
moft able BOXERS within the AUTHOR's Time.

By Capt. JOHN GODFREY.

LONDON:
Printed for the AUTHOR, by [T. Robinson at Milton's]
Head [opposite St. Clement's Church in the Strand]
[Maiden Lane] MDCCXLVII. [Covent Garden]

Price — 1-6

TO HIS
ROYAL HIGHNESS
THE
D U K E.

SIR,

I BEG Leave, with the profoundeſt Humility, to lay the following Eſſay at Your Royal Highneſs's Feet. That Part of it, which treats of the Back-Sword, I have proved (I flatter myſelf) to be of ſingular Advantage in the Army; upon which Account I would willingly preſume, it may not be altogether unacceptable to a Prince of Your Royal Highneſs's military Genius. The other Exerciſes I have deſcanted upon muſt be confeſſed to be of inferior Conſequence; but the meaneſt of them, in my poor Opinion, greatly contributes to inure the common People to Bravery; and to encourage that truly *Britiſh* Spirit, which was the Glory of

A 2

our

DEDICATION.

our Anceſtors, and is ſurprizingly reviving under the Influence of your Royal Highneſs's heroic and gallant Behaviour. Few Generals have appeared *Conſpicuous* ſo early. You have, Great Sir, begun glorioufly; You cannot fail of imitating the Illuſtrious Houſe from whence you are defcended, and going on fuccefsfully to Perfection. That intrepid Valour; That admirably wife Conduct, which have diſtinguiſhed your Royal Highneſs againſt his Majeſty's Enemies at Home, will one Day become formidable to thofe Abroad, and check the Infolence of the grand Diſturber of the Peace and Liberties of *Europe.*

I am, SIR,

With the higheſt Admiration, and the warmeſt Zeal,

Your ROYAL HIGHNESS'S

Moſt Obedient, and

Moſt Devoted Servant,

JOHN GODFREY.

THE

PREFACE.

FOR several Years I have been advised, and even importuned by my Friends, to publish something upon the SWORD; but have from Time to Time declined it, from a Diffidence of my Abilities to put my Thoughts, however just they may be in respect to the SWORD, into a Dress fit for publick Appearance. The Strength of Self-Love, and that Vanity, which hardly any Man is entirely free from, has at length got the better of my Temerity, and prevailed upon me to put Pen to Paper.

I think, I have had some Knowledge of the Theory and Practice of the SWORD: The following Reasons may be some Excuse for my Conceit. If I am mistaken, no Man living has been more abominably abused by Flattery; for I have for many Years been fed with that Notion from the Town, and have been told that I could execute what I knew, and

A 2

give

give better Reasons for what I did in the
SWORD, than most Men, by Men of Rank so far
above me, that it is scarce to be supposed, they
would ever debase themselves by idly flattering one
so insignificant. I believe it will be farther acknow-
ledged, that I have a considerable Time supported
this Opinion of myself by proving it upon all, who
were willing to dispute it with me. I have pur-
chased my Knowledge in the BACK-SWORD with
many a broken Head, and Bruise in every Part of
me. I chose to go mostly to FIG, and exercise
with him; partly, as I knew him to be the ablest
Master, and partly, as he was of a rugged Temper,
and would spare no Man, high or low, who took
up a Stick against him. I bore his rough Treat-
ment with determined Patience, and followed him
so long, that FIG, at last, finding he could not
have the beating of me at so cheap a Rate as usual,
did not shew such Fondness for my Company. This
is well known by Gentlemen of distinguished Rank,
who used to be pleased in setting us together.

I have tryed with all the eminent Masters since
FIG's Time, and I believe, made them sensible of
what I could do; and it has been so publickly proved, that I cannot think any one will deny the Fact.

I

PREFACE.

I have followed chiefly the Practice of the BACK-SWORD, because Conceit cannot so readily be cured with the File in the Small, as with the Stick in that: For the *Argumentum bastinandi* is very strong and convincing; and though a Man may dispute the full Hit of a File, yet if he is knocked down with a Stick, he will hardly get up again and say, it *just brushed him*. This has been my Reason for preferring the BACK-SWORD; but still I think I understand the true Principles, and am tolerably well versed in the Exercise of the other; and indeed they are so closely connected, that what will answer in the former, will rarely disappoint in the latter.

☞ I have been informed, since the finishing of this Preface, that there are Pirates watching at the Harbour's Mouth, to snap up this poor Prize as soon as she comes out. In *December* last a Friend of mine happened to be at the *Bull and Gate* in *Holbourn*, when there came in a Printer elevated with Liquor; and as Men in those Circumstances are pretty forward, he immediately began to prattle, not suspecting the Gentleman had any Acquaintance with me; and told him that he was just come from dining with a certain Fencing-Master, who had a Treatise upon the SWORD ready for the Press; but they waited only for the Publication of my Book, to pick

out

PREFACE.

out of it what they liked, and force the Sale againſt mine, by conſiderably underſelling me. This Fencing-Maſter has a Partner, who, I hope, has no Hand in it; nay alſo hope, that it may be but a Story worked up in the fermenting Brain of a drunken Man. But in caſe he has ſuch a Deſign, *That Maſter*, when he looks into my CHARACTERS, if he has one Grain of Honeſty in him, muſt be ſtruck with Shame and Deteſtation of himſelf.

N. B. *The Printer was coming into the* Bull and Gate, *as I was going out; and his ſeeing me was, I preſume, the Cauſe of his falling ſo directly upon this Subject.*

THE
THEORY
OF THE
SWORD.

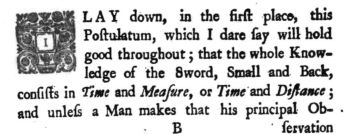 LAY down, in the firſt place, this Poſtulatum, which I dare ſay will hold good throughout; that the whole Knowledge of the Sword, Small and Back, conſiſts in *Time* and *Meaſure*, or *Time* and *Diſtance*; and unleſs a Man makes that his principal Ob-

fervation, he never can fucceed in his Defigns
but by chance, which, though a poor Dependance,
is all that moft Swords-Men go upon.

I will endeavour to explain what I mean by *Time*
and *Meafure*. *Time*, relative to the Sword, I call
an inftantaneous Agreement between your Eye and
your Adverfary's *Point*, when to act. I cannot
imagine, what they could mean, who recommended
the watching your Adverfary's Eye, which is fo apt
to deceive you, while you are trufting to it. I believe that Practice to be fo much out of the Quef-
tion now, among Men who are any Kind of Judges,
that I look upon a Refutation of it as unneceffary.
There is more to be faid for the Wrift and Arm,
and even Leg, than for the Eye: None of thefe
will, or can deceive you, if you are a nice and juft
Obferver of the *Point*; but muft vary their Pofitions
according to that. The Reafon why I am an Advo-
cate for the *Point*, is becaufe, as it is fo much
nearer to your Eye, every minute Motion of it is
more perceptible; and as the Arm and Wrift are
the mechanical Caufes of it, they muft anfwer to
the Effect, and that Effect is nearer to your Ken
than the Caufe. This I take to be a mathematical
Proof.

Secondly,

[3]

Secondly, As I lay the whole Strefs upon *Time*, (and I believe all who in the Practice have fucceeded, muft confefs this to be right,) I affert, that the Exactnefs of *Time* appears by the *Point*, whofe minute Motion and Variation, gives you more Advantage of *Time*, from the unavoidable and infenfible Tremor of it, caufed by the Extenfion of the Arm. For your *Time* may be fo nicely divided, that every Tremor of the *Point* will give you a fair Invitation to your Oppofer's Body. It is therefore called the *Feeble*, and certainly the Part you ought to attack. That it is weaker according to its Extenfion, we need not go about to prove: But let us obferve, that according to its Extenfion, it muft produce a proportionable Tremor; which, as it has a phyfical Caufe, can never be overcome or difguifed by the pureft Conftitution: and that *Time*, from the watchful Obfervation of the trembling *Point*, will (to be humoroufly difpofed, though not much in the Humour to play with Words) carry the *Point*. As I faid before, you need not look at any thing but the *Point*; this, in courfe, carries you along the Line to the Wrift, which muft move and change with the Sword, as it is the Caufe of the *Point*'s Variation.

B 2

The

The next Confideration is *Meafure*, or *Diftance*.

Meafure, in refpect of the Sword, is the mutual *Diftance* between your Adverfary and you, and a juft Menfuration of that *Diftance*, without which you will always be liable to be deceived by your Adverfary's Sword, and mifcarry with your own. This *Meafure*, which we cannot enlarge upon without ftepping into the Practice, will always be a fure Guide to you, both in the offenfive and defenfive Part, as we fhall evidently prove in the practical Part, which we therefore enter upon immediately; for in our Opinion, by dwelling longer upon the Theory, we fhould only render ourfelves more obfcure and unintelligible.

The Practice of the SMALL *and* BACK-SWORD.

WE muft diftinguifh them and treat of them feparately, or elfe we fhall not be able to point out their proximate Caufes and Effects. We begin with the *Small-Sword*, which we muft allow to be the neareft Inlet to the relative Arts, and when

when we are upon the *Back-Sword*, their near Affinity will appear still more clearly. I must again bring in my *Time* and *Measure*, and lay them down as the first Stones in the Building. This Principle is the Basis and Foundation of the Whole, without which it cannot be supported; but upon the Justness of that, you may carry your Works as high as you please. But then I would have no Carving or Wrought-work, which, wherever it is found, always weakens the Structure. The plainest Work may be laid down to be the strongest, and though Fashions are titillating for a Time, even to Sense, yet in the End Nature's Taste will prove triumphant. This is a Kind of Digreffion, the Admiffion of which we crave for the prefent, and in due Courfe, fhall further explain Matters. To proceed gradually in the Practice, after having laid down the Foundation to the whole Superftructure, we muft now mention the *Body*, the Pofition of which is certainly moft effential. We need not explain what we mean by that, fince it is obvious, that the common Pofture with the Sword, deprives you of a great deal more of the Body's *Meafure*, than the natural Pofture without the Sword. But then this *Meafure* given you by the undefigning Body, how much may it not be diminifhed by an
artful

artful Posture. The *Body*, the more it is contracted, (or, if I may say, absorb'd into the Line) gives your Adversary the less Object to offend, and also you the more advancing Power over him. The smaller his *Mark* is, the harder it is for him to hit; and what is the trifling Difference between the Nearness of your Body to him by this Position, to the Comparison of the Advantage you give him in your whole breasted Body? Then if the Position brings your right Breast nearer to him, it also brings your *Point* nearer to him, (supposing you make a proper Use of your Arm;) and in proportion to that, he must be obliged to alter his *Distance*. We will suppose the human Body (one with another) to be about twelve Inches over; that *Mark* I will engage, by a proper Posture, to reduce to four Inches. What Difference then must not that Reduction to a third Part, make towards my Safety? At the same Time, the more I bring my Body to this Position, the more direct the Line of my Arm and Sword must be; consequently my *Cover* must the closer, and therefore my Adversary's Designs frustrated and rendered abortive. So much for the *Body*, upon which your Safety greatly depends.

The

The Pofition of your *Sword-Arm*, is alfo a very effential Point. Doubtlefs, the ftraighter that is, the fecurer your Line is; but you cannot fo readily come to Action, get upon your Parade, or execute your *Thruft*, from an Arm quite ftraight, as when a little contracted. But then you muft take great Care of bending it too much; for certainly the more the Arm is bent, the more your Line is broken, and confequently the more your Body is expofed to your Adverfary's Defigns. The left Arm, which I have found infignificant in moft Fencers, I take to contribute not a little for you. The Extenfion of that is a very great Balance to your Body, and we fhall find it, upon trying, as difficult to Fence with the left Arm down, as a Man, who ufes not a Pole, would to dance upon the Rope without extending his Arms. But then that Arm I would have extended backwards, and not (as I oftner fee on the contrary) raifed forward. I think the Beauty of the Pofture is ftrangely disfigured by it; and I dare fay a Painter would not be tempted with its Attitude; and that all Fencers will allow that they cannot help being pleafed with a fymmetrical Pofture, and growing partial to the Performance from a fine Attitude. This raifing the Arm and bringing it forward, as to the Sight, has an unpleafing, crippled and diftorted

Look;

Look; and when I fee a Man's Arm in fuch a Pofture, I cannot help charitably wifhing him in *Chelfea*
College. As to ufe——certainly, the more your left
Arm is brought forward, the more that Part of the
Body you have, by your proper Line, hid from your
Oppofer, is brought back for his Sword, and I can
conceive no Advantage in it, except it be a Defign
to make ufe of it in a *Parry*. That Practice I am
utterly againft, and though all the while I write, I
write and think with a due Submiffion to my
Readers, and Deference to fuperior Judgements, I
own I am fo confident of its being manifeftly bad,
that I think it needlefs to advance any Reafons
againft it.

Let us now treat of the *Legs*.

If your *Feet* do not form a right Line, your Body
proportionably muft be turned out of the Line.
But this I fhall not enlarge upon; for I do not defign this Treatife, to form a Swords-Man out of a
Man quite ignorant of it, but as an Offer and Recommendation to thofe who are Judges: Nor do I
defign it for fcholaftic methodical Rules to learn by,
fuch as a Teacher is obliged to advance to his Pupils;
but an expatiating upon the Art, with an Endeavour

to

to weed it of its formal Miftakes, and fupply it
with fuch Practices, as I think will hold good upon
all Trials. Others may differ as much as they pleafe
about the Weight and Strefs put upon either *Leg*
more than the other. I am of Opinion, that the
Diftribution of the Duty laid upon each *Leg* ought
to be equal; and the more equally they fhare in the
Weight, I will venture to fay the Body will be fo
much the more fupported. This is a kind of mathematical Theory. But let us examine into the
confequential Practice, by the Difadvantage of laying a greater Strefs upon one *Leg* than the other, or
the Advantage to be expected from the Strength
accruing from the proper Weight given to both. If
too great a Strefs lie upon the left *Leg*, your Retreat muft be obvioufly the more unready, and
weaker; if upon the Right, you are crimped of
(if I may ufe the Word) and checked in your advancing. If the greater Share of Weight lie upon
the Right, the left *Leg* muft take that Share off,
before you can advance; and fo, *vice verfa*, the
Right muft act for the Left in the Retreat. But
then this is the Lofs of your *Time*, upon which every
thing depends; whereas by the equilibrial Weight
upon the *Legs*, that *Time* is faved. Here your *Body*
will be equally fupported, and therefore ftronger

C   and

and steadier; but by the recovering and shifting in the other Way, the Motion of the Body must be so much greater, that your Arm is more likely to be thrown out of the Line.

Thus much as to the Swords-Man's Position.

Let us now enter upon the executive Parts. The *Parade* is one of the most material Points in Action; without being Master of which, you will never be safe from a well timed *Thrust*, or come readily to the Return, if you happen to *parry* it. The true *Parade* is the Office of the Wrist, and the less that is helped by the Arm, the more faithful it is; but if the Arm decoys away the Wrist, they will both conspire against you. Upon a narrow *Parade*, from the frugal Turn of the Wrist, depends most of your Advantage; but if your Arm makes it profuse, you will be liable to the grossest Feints of your Adversary; and you will not only never be able to hit him safely, but lose your Time, and, like a Traveller, who is got into the wrong Road, be obliged to come back into the true, before you can get to the desired Place.

The

The *Thurst*, in itself confidered, ought to be as faithful to the Line as poffible. This is fo obvious, that I think it needlefs to dwell upon it. As I faid before, I never propofed to go on gradually, as a Teacher, but to write to Swords-Men, to offer what I think is neceffary, to lop off what is unneceffary, and explode what is deftructive to the Art. I can allow but of three *Thrufts*; whatever elfe is done, is only an Emanation from thofe Sources. That *Thruft* called the *Flanconade*, I pronounce an Anathema upon, as being eafily proved to be the moft lewd and vile Debaucher of the Art, the Dignity of which confifts chiefly in its generous Allowance of a proportionable Chance to the weak Man. The other *Thrufts* depend upon a timely Swiftnefs moftly: Though to fay, that equal Knowledge with more Strength has not the Advantage, would be prepof-terous, as certainly the greater the Velocity is, the greater the giving Strength muft be. But there is a kind of Supplenefs in the Joints, and Spring in the Wrift, partly natural in Mankind, and partly ac-quired by Ufe and Exercife. This you do not al-ways find in proportion to Man's Strength; and it is what fome Men, with all their Practice, will never attain to. I have feen fome, and doubt not, but it has been obferved by feveral others, who with a Body

and

and Arm almoſt ſtrong enough to fling another over
a Wall, with a Stick in the Hand could not hit a
Blow half ſo hard and ſmart, as another could with
half their Strength; they always ſtriking down like
a Woman with a ſtraight Arm, without raiſing or
jirking the Wriſt. Now I ſay, that a weak Man,
either by Nature or more Practice than a ſtrong
Man, may be ſwifter, and in courſe ſtronger in his
Thruſts, and his *Parades*, by that natural Supple-
neſs, or acquired Spring. He therefore may ſet
up for a Candidate in the Art, and make a proportionable Intereſt in it. But he ſtands a wretched
Chance in attempting the *Flanconade* upon a ſtronger
Man, and runs little riſk, if ſuperior Strength dares
it upon him. That *Thruſt* can never be compaſſed,
but by main Force upon the moſt feeble, and at
the ſame Time moſt ignorant Patient. Nothing leſs
is required, to give any Hopes of Succeſs in it, but
the Strength of a Giant againſt a Pigmy. And even
that vaſt Superiority of Strength muſt fail, if the
weak Man is induſtrious in his *Parade*; for I will
venture to ſay, that there is not the tenth Part of
the Strength required in the *Parade*, that there is in
the *Thruſt*; and if that *Parade* be duly timed (upon which every thing of the Sword depends, and
yet diſtinct from Strength) no Strength will carry it,
and

and the very *Parry* is a certain unfought-for *Thrust*, which muft go furer into your Adverfary's Body, than any other *Thruft* you can make, and never can deceive you, becaufe his Sword colleagues againft him, and by the twifted Lock his binding File has formed, carries you unerringly in.

The Art we had from the *French*; no *Flanconade* was thought of for fome Time; but upon finding us very apt Scholars, and being willing to be our diftinguifhed Mafters, they brought in the *Flanconade* and many tawdry Embroideries, which they are as famous for inventing, as, I am forry to fay, we are degenerate enough to imitate, and even mimick. Pity! that we fhould be fo fond of imitating a Nation, who have always been deceiving us. Roufe then, thou noble Britifh Spirit! (for fure no Time more calling than the prefent) lift up thy brave fronted Head above thefe dandling Actions, and become thy wonted felf! Love thy King, love thy Country; ftay thy Heart in thefe, and thou art fafe.

Thus I take my hearty farewel of the *Flanconade:*

The three *Thrufts* are, *Infide*, *Outfide* and *Seconde*. By the two former I fhall be eafily underftood,

ftood, and would chufe to avoid the Pain of being
in the Fafhion to parrot Words and ape Actions.
The latter I will retain between the Trouble of finding out a Word that will go down with Prepoffef-
fion, and the Fear of being condemned for coining
Words, and will call it yet *Seconde*.

The common Practice of the *Infide* I have no Ob-
jections againft; but would recommend great Care
not to turn the Wrift that way too much (as it is
too often practifed) for fear of lofing your Line.
The general Practice of the *Outfide* I object againft,
which is the turning your Wrift to the Left, and fo,
in courfe bring the Back of your Hand upward,
which muft throw your Point (that is moft in a Line
with your Thumb) to the Left, while it is defigned
for the Right; but turning your Wrift to the Right,
and bringing your Palm upwards, reverfely carries
your Point into the Body.

The *Seconde* is an excellent *Thruft*, and I am of
Opinion, that if it be proportionably well made
with the others, it will oftner execute; becaufe you
will not be fo apt to flip out of your Line with this
as in the other two, which often happens in too much
Eagernefs to be home with your *Thruft*. But in this,

your

your Adverfary's Sword, which differs more in the *Parade* than the others, proves a better Guide, and fupports you in your Paffage. In this *Thruft* I would recommend the Point to be well elevated, that you may allow for its Fall: For as the Arm defcribes a Kind of Curve when you make it, it is very apt to light below the Body for want of a due raifed Point. In the other *Thrufts* it is dangerous to raife it too much, becaufe they being fo much higher may eafily pafs over the Body. But the *Seconde* being fo much lower, and in its paffing upwards backed and fupported by your Adverfary's Blade, threatens you with very little Danger that way.

I have done with the *Thrufts*, and I prefume, I have laid down the true Principles of the Art.

The reft are moftly Excrefcencies or difeafed Irruptions. Such as I fear your *Difarms, Vaults, Batters, &c.* are; in which I think any Body that duly obferves it, will find you oftner to mifcarry than fucceed. Your *Vaults* I have always found to be moft dangerous, and we need only give this Reafon, that the Body, which certainly muft move proportionably with the left Leg, differing widely from

the

the Body's Motion, attending the right *Leg* with a
Longe in the ſtraight Line, and which is ſo much
the greater Weight than the Arm, cannot be moved
within the ſame Time with that which is lighter.
The *Diſarms*, by ſtepping in upon the *Parry*, or *Bind*,
may be ſometimes practiſed, but never but with
great Advantage of Skill and Strength. But the
Lord have Mercy on the battering, twiſting Diſ-
armer, falling foul upon the cunning wary Slipper.
To conclude, I would make this, I think, neceſſary
Obſervation, that the ſame Awe ought to be paid to
the File, as to the Sword, whoſe Repreſentative it
ſurely is. Nothing ought to be attempted by the
one, that would be feared with the other; and if
we think thoſe petulant Familiarities, which are
uſed with the File, dare not be with the Sword, we
may lopp and prune the Art of many noxious
Branches.

I cannot help taking notice, that the left-handed
Man has the Advantage over the right-handed, upon an equal Footing; becauſe as there are more
right-handed, than left-handed, the latter muſt be
more uſed to the former, than the former to the latter. For my Part I own, that in both Small and
Back-Sword, I would rather contend with the right-
handed

handed Man with more Judgment, than the other with lefs. I dare fay no Body would chufe to be left-handed, and therefore would propofe a Way to put a ftop to that undefired Race, and fubmit to the Public whether it bears the Face of Reafon. The Nurfe carries the Child in the left Arm; the Confequence of that is, it's right Arm is confined and the left at liberty to play and exercife; and I believe it will be allowed that the Child, in its Infancy, is moft of the Day in the Nurfe's Arms. If accuftomed to that Habit, fo long as till it can go alone, no wonder of it's continuing to ufe the left Arm; and I am confident moft would be left-handed, if they were not by the Parent's Care broke of that Habit after they are parted from the Nurfe. But let the Child be carried in the right Arm, I engage he will fcarcely turn left-handed; for that Arm next to the Nurfe's Body is certainly in a great Meafure confined and rendered inactive. But to return to our Purpofe.

I have fometimes found the hanging Guard of the Back-Sword anfwer very well in the Small. I would not recommend it to be ufed againft a regular Fencer; but there are a great many Men, who by their Awkwardnefs will puzzle a good Fencer. A Gentle-

G   man

man of my Acquaintance exercifes very much in the Small and Back. I have been more hit by his bufy, buftling irregular Way, than by the beft Fencers. I have been fo often hit by him in an unaccountable Manner, that I took it in my Head at laft to try that Guard. I fucceeded fo well with it, that I puzzled him afterwards as much as he did me, and hit him much fafer with my Thrufts.

But then whenever we have recourfe to the *Hanging* Guard, I would recommend great Care that your Adverfary feels not your *Feeble*, becaufe it muft be weaker in that Guard, from the twifting and ftraining of the Mufcles, caufed by the irregular Curve your Arm defcribes.

I have now done with the Small-Sword, and fhall only do Juftice to the Merits of two or three Mafters.

I have a very great Opinion of the Abilities of Mr. *Brent*, Partner with Mr. *Barney Hill*. Sure no two in Conjunction could fupport and ftrengthen the Art more than thefe two Gentlemen.

The

The one's folid Way of Teaching, which his Age does not interfere with, and the other's Prime of Strength, Activity and true Judgment in affaulting, certainly muft bring forth excellent Swords-Men.

One of the fineft Matches I ever faw, was between Mr. *Brent* and Mr. *Dubois*. The beautiful Defigns I obferved between them gave me extreme Delight. This *Dubois* is one of the moft charming Figures upon the Floor I ever beheld. His genteel neat Motions, and Mr. *Brent*'s firm Foot, majeftic Body, and graceful Arm were oppofite Electrics to my Fancy. If the different Excellencies of thefe two were united, they would make one inimitable Swords-Man.

Let us not omit to do Juftice to that long ftanding able Mafter, Mr. *Martin*, Senior. He muft be allowed to be a confummate Teacher, and no Body has done his Scholars more Juftice than Mr. *Martin*. His Son is a delightful Fencer, and his Merit is the more extraordinary, becaufe he maintains it, by Dint of Judgment, through all the Difadvantages of a weak Conftitution.

Let

Let it not be faid that I think there are not any more Mafters, becaufe I make no further mention of them. Doubtlefs there are many more deferving ones in Town ; but I have not happened upon the Opportunities of obferving them fo much as thefe.

I now proceed to the Back-Sword,

As this is founded upon the fame Principles with the other, I fhall direƈtly enter upon the Praƈtice. Here every thing will hold good that has been faid of the Body in the Small-Sword, which may be contraƈted into this Poftulatum ; That the more of your Body you hide from your Adverfary by an artful Pofture, the more you deprive him of his *Mark*; and, for the fame Reafon I gave in the Small-Sword, the more you are in the Line, the fafer you are.

The true Pofture of the Small-Sword is a fafe one in the Back-Sword ; and if I were to form a thorough Back-Swords Man, I would have him learn firft the Small-Sword : From that he fteps into the other fo eafily and readily, with the true guiding Principles he has acquired, that the double Doƈtrine I can hardly think a round-about Way. The fparing Turn of the Wrift in *Parrys*, the clofe *Cover* and
the

the narrow *Stops* will, fave you that Time, which is fquandered away in the common taught *Parades* by the Back-Sword Mafters. It will curtail your teaching, and introduce you to the Art a much fhorter Way. What has been faid of the Arms and Legs in the other, will equally hold good in this. There is a common Objection againft this Affertion, in refpect to the Legs. They fay, you lay more Weight upon your left Leg, that you may the more readily flip your right from your Adverfary's Cut. But I abide by the Doctrine of an equal Diftribution of Weight (or as near as you can give it) to both Legs. I have always found it to anfwer, and upon my laying too great a Strefs upon my left Leg, in order to flip my right, it has been fo weak that I have been ready to fall backwards upon lifting up my right, and by that ftruggle to recover, have loft my Time, on which all my Expectations depend, and by it's due obfervance, all my Defigns muft be executed.

Here are four Guards, *viz. Infide, Outfide, Medium,* and *Hanging.* This is the common Acceptation; but I think miftakingly. For I do not fee why there fhould be any more underftood by a Guard, than one true covering Pofture in the Line.

The

The *Medium* is the Small-Sword Pofture, and that alone may properly be called a Guard; which I 'define to be an abfolute defenfive Pofition, independent of your Adverfary's Motions; but the other are occafional Motions produced by your Adverfary's Defigns.

The *Infide* and *Outfide* are proper Poftures to pitch to, according to your executive Intentions; but then they are acting Parts of the Sword, and improperly called Guards, whereby fhould be fomething paffively fixed, and altered only into Action, as Occafion offers. The *Hanging* may with more Truth be called a Guard than the other two. But then it is (if I may fay) a Guard too paffive, becaufe you cannot fo readily get from it into Action, as from the other.

The Beauty of the Small-Sword Pofture is, that it is a true Guard or Cover from your Enemy, and a Readinefs to attack and offend him. But a Guard without a Power of offending, is fhutting yourfelf up in a Caftle from your Adverfary, or running away from him.

The

The *Hanging* Guard is a very good Guard to pitch
to, when you are gathered upon, and preſſed by
your Adverſary. But then it is owing to your want
of the proper Guard, that you are reduced to this
ſhift, and no better than a Retreat, when your Lines
are broken. I always pity the Man, when I ſee him
upon that Guard, and am apt to ſtep up to his Adverſary and intercede for Mercy. But whenever I
ſee a fine, eaſy, compoſed, confidently looking *Point*,
I put extraordinary Faith in it.

Let us now come to the *Cuts* and *Stops*. There
is one eſſential Thing, I think I ſhould have brought
in before, and which, neceſſary as it is, is much
neglected and overlooked, and that is the Manner
of holding the Sword. I may be excuſed for omit-
ting it, becauſe, as I ſaid, I do not propoſe to breed
up a Swords-Man, but write to Swords-Men. But
this Miſtake is ſo common, even among good
Swords-Men, that it calls for due Correction; and
whether that Correction, or any paſt, or to come, be
juſt, I ſubmiſſively offer to my judicious Readers.
If they are demonſtrative, they will be clear to all
Judgments; if not, I fall by them. If they be
mathematical Proofs, they will be evincing to the

Man

Man of Senfe, though he be not a Swords-Man ; and
if they appear fo to Senfe, I fhall never trouble my
Head, whether they are accepted by the Obftinate
and Tenacious.

The common Way of holding the Sword is with
a kind of globular Hand, that is, all the Fingers
and the Thumb making a Circle round the Sword.
The Confequence of which is, that when you come
to make your Cut, your Gripe moves and flips round
your Palm, and you lofe your directing Edge. But
let the Sword be held with your Thumb, raifed upon the Surface and extended in a ftraight Line, you
will never fail to carry an Edge. For the want of
this Obfervation, where I have feen one Blow judi-
cioufly given in Time, upon the Adverfary's Open,
execute the Defign, I have feen ten loft by falling
on the Flat. The *Infide* and the *Outfide* Throws
are both very fafe. I give the Preference to the *Infide* ; becaufe it goes with a furer Edge, and may be
made with more Strength and Velocity.

This is very obfervable in Battles fought upon the
Stage, where you will find all the *Infide* Cuts to be
much deeper and feverer than the *Outfide*. It muft
be allowed alfo, that they are more likely to hit
the

the Face, which being fo much more tender than the
Head, will fooner carry the Battle. Indeed, the
Outfide Throw I would recommend for the Head and
Face, when your Adverfary makes to your Leg; it
keeps clearer of his Blade, and if well timed, fel-
dom meets with Interruption; but efpecially if it
be made flanting, with a Kind of a back Sweep,
which, if your Antagonift be not very wary and
quick in his Recover, muft hit him in the Face,
and this fweeping Turn carries a direct Edge. But
in the whole, I fhould chufe to be moft familiar
with the *Infide*, as I take it to be more faithful to
the Line, and you certainly can recover quicker and
more readily from it. Nature feems to have made
it more a Friend to Time: For I believe it will be
allowed, that a Man naturally can make an *Infide*
Blow quicker and eafier than an *Outfide*, and certainly oftner, before the Wrift is fatigued, as the
Turn of it that way is not fo great a Strain upon
the Mufcles, as the other; and I dare fay a Man's
Arm will be fooner ftrained and weakened by ftrong
Blows to the *Outfide*, than to the *Infide*, becaufe in
the *Infide* Blow the Mufcles act in a true Line of
Direction, but in the other are contorted or twifted,
and their Power thereby weakened; for it is well
known by every Anatomift fkilled in mufcular Mo-

E   tion,

tion, that the two extreme Parts of a Mufcle muft anfwer a true Line of Direction, before the Mufcle can act with Power.

This all belongs to the offenfive Part; but then in the defenfive Part, the *Infide Stops* are readier, fafer, and fnugger under the *Cover*. Doubtlefs, when a Man makes an *Outfide* Blow at you, you muft ftop it from the *Outfide*, or the *Hanging*, which is a kind of *Outfide*; but then the *Infide Stop*, which is moftly practifed for the *Cover* of the *Infide* of the Arm or Wrift, and the *Infide* of the Face, will alfo, if it be well timed, ftop a Blow made full down to the Head, as fafe as the St. *George's* and *Hanging* Guard, which are generally ufed in ftopping full Throws at the Head. Befides, as I have recommended fighting from the *Infide*, which is neareft to the *Medium*, notwithftanding the *Medium* has it's Name from a Notion of it's being in the Middle between them, I affert that you are more in the Line with it, your *Stops* are more juft, under better *Cover*, and allow of a readier and narrower Return.

I have tried them all; I always found myfelf fafer upon the *Infide*, when preffed upon (for the *Hanging* Guard I always defpifed) and to fuccced better in my Attempts upon my Adverfary.   The

The moft dangerous Cut in the Sword to your
Oppofer (and which generally carries the keeneft
Edge) is the *Infide* Blow at the Wrift. This is far
readier, and nearer to it, and when hit, more effectual
than the *Outfide*, and certainly the Cut anfwers your
Ends more than any other, becaufe your Enemy is
difabled at once. Any other Cut he may bear for a
while, and have a Chance of hitting you, if he con-
tinues to fight a little longer; but the Inftant you
hit him in the *Infide* of the Wrift, your Victory is
fecure. Another fubftantial, and I think, mathematical Reafon for efpoufing it, is, becaufe the
Wrift of your Adverfary is that Part of him, which,
while it is the moft dangerous to him if wounded,
in refpect to the Battle, is alfo the neareft to you,
and confequently the fafeft for you to attack; becaufe, hit, or mifs, on account of your Diftance from
him, you are fafer from his Return. Nothing can
be fafer in the Back-Sword, than lying firm to a low
Infide, and waiting for the other's moving; the Mo-
ment he raifes his Wrift is your Opportunity to go
to it, and if you act according to that due Obfervation of *Time*, you cannot fail of meeting his Wrift.
You may pitch your *Infide* Pofture fo wide to the
Outfide, as to hide all the *Outfide*, and leave him
nothing but an *Infide* Mark; and yet, though your

Infide

Inside is more open by it, you are in less Danger, because you are sure your *Outside* is lost to him, and you have nothing to watch but your *Inside*; while you lie to that with a ready raised Wrist, your Blade will always be Time enough to meet his Wrist; which must execute prodigiously, because there is the conjunctive Force of his Throw and yours meeting together.

There is one thing I would advance, which I judge highly necessary, and ought to be treated of as a most useful Point in the Sword; and that is, what we call breaking *Measure*. This breaking *Measure* is certainly very material; but then the Man who practiseth it, ought to be an exact Judge of *Time*. It will succeed greatly in the Sword, both Back and Small, but in this Attempt of meeting your Adversary's Wrist, it is most significant: For by that little Contraction of your Body, which perhaps does not make an Inch Difference in *Measure*, you will secure yourself from your Adversary's Blade, which by his Strength in the Throw, or your not so exactly timing it, as you ought, might bend over to your Face, though you meet him in the Wrist. Here (if I would ever encourage it) I would advise moving a little, but very little, out of the Line. It is a Kind of *Vault*,

I

I own ; but far unlike the others I mutinied againſt in the Small-Sword. The others are deſigned to put the Body out of your Adverſary's Line, which certainly takes up too much Time to avoid an active Arm; but in this the Body moves little or nothing, and it depends chiefly on throwing your Head back behind your Hilt, to allow for the bending over of his Sword, which certainly it muſt do in ſome Meaſure, becauſe you meet his ſoft unreſiſting Wriſt, and not his hard reverberating Blade; and even if you meet his Blade towards his Hilt, it muſt proportionably bend over, more than if you ſtop him towards the Point. This Throw at the *Inſide* of the Wriſt I pronounce to be the ſafeſt, and moſt effectual in the whole Sword. As it will fit this Place beſt, I will anticipate my Characters of the MASTERs, by bringing in one *Perkins* an *Iriſhman*. The Man certainly was a true Swords-Man, but his Age made him ſo ſtiff and ſlow in his Action, that he could not execute all that his Judgment put him upon; yet, by Dint of that, he made up for his Inactivity. He always, at firſt ſetting out, pitched to this Poſture, lying, as I ſaid before, low to the *Inſide*, ſo wide as to hide all the *Outſide*, with his Wriſt ſo ready raiſed, that no body knew what to do with him. I have ſeen FIG, in Battles with him, ſtand

in

in a kind of Confusion, not knowing which way to move : For as F I G offered to move, the old Man would also move so warily upon the Catch, that he would disappoint him in most of his Designs. Whatever Attempts are made upon a Man in this Posture so dangerous to attack, ought to be made below his Wrist, and for my part, in this Case I should go with a straight drawing Drop upon his Thigh, neither to the *Inside* nor *Outside* of it, but directly down in a Line from the *Medium* ; because, first, there is that Time saved, which is required in the Turn of your Wrist ; and secondly, your Adversary, who has been only waiting for it, is disappointed in his Design, and can do nothing, but attempt to drop down and follow your Arm; but in order to do that, must lose his Time in shifting his Wrist. Many a Time when I have been engaged with the Stick, with an Opponent who was so very ready with the Slip of his Leg and the Throw at my Head, (which is done in one and the same Motion) I have found myself in so much Danger, that I durst not go down to the *Outside* of his Leg ; but in going down with a drawing Blade in a straight Line, from the *Medium*, I have deceived him, and hit him a smart Blow upon the Foot about the Toes. This Method will save me from my Antagonist, though the other

will

will not, both from leffening the Time (which is apparent in the Motion) and likewife, from ſhort-ning the *Meaſure*, as much as his Foot is more within the *Meaſure* of your ſtraight Line, than the *Outſide* of his Leg, which makes a ſurpriſing Difference in both *Time* and *Meaſure*. This brings us to treat of the going down to the Leg.

It is done after receiving, or moving. As I write to thoſe who underſtand ſomething of the Sword, theſe Sword Terms will be underſtood: Receiving is the ſtopping our Adverſary's Blow firſt, and then going to his Leg: Moving, is going down without receiving, but taking care before you go down, to move his Sword out of the Line.

Maſters moſtly recommend the receiving firſt, as the ſafeſt way. I am a Friend to the other, which, whether it be thought as ſafe or not, I am ſure is more likely to catch the other's Leg, becauſe it is done in leſs Time. And beſides, in point of ſafety, I always found it anſwer full as well as the other; and in my Opinion, a Man that has moved his Ad-verſary truly, before he goes down to his Leg, is leſs likely to be hit above in going down, becauſe there is leſs Notice and Intelligence given of your

Deſign,

Defign; and it requires a much nicer Judgment in your Opponent, to diftinguifh here, than it is for him to be apprifed of your going down, after you have ftopped him above. The Action is fo common after receiving, that when a Man makes a full Blow at your Head, he, even undefignedly, fhifts his Leg back to avoid your Return at it. But it is a diffi-cult Matter for him to provide and guard againft your little or no notice-giving Movings and going down. Without taking up unneceffary Time in ex-amining the different Ways in going to the Leg, I pronounce it beft from the *Infide*, by which you can eafier get under your Adverfary's Blade, and the Turn of your Wrift from the *Infide* to the *Outfide* is a nearer Way and carries your Blade more in, than from any of the *Outfides* (for the *Hanging* and St. *George* are properly *Outfides*) in going down from which your Elbow is to the Right, and in courfe. your Blade to the Left, and fo much farther from the Leg. In the Attempt from the *Infide* your El-bow is the oppofite Way, and your Blade goes in towards the Leg, and when it hits, gives a much more dangerous Cut, on account of the drawing Stroke, which certainly is palpably more fo, than from the *Outfide*. Here the breaking *Meafure* is of excellent Ufe, and more wanted than any where

elfe;

elfe; becaufe your Head and whole Body is brought
fo much nearer to your Adverfary's Sword; therefore your Arm and your Head fhould, if poffible,
have one oppofite Motion, to which by Practice you
may foon bring yourfelf. What I mean is this; when
your Arm approaches your Adverfary, your Head
fhould turn from him, and you ought to fall inftantaneoufly back to the Left, with your other Parts
out of the Line of his Sword.

This breaking *Meafure* is moft ufeful and fafe in
both Small and Back-Sword, becaufe, *Meafure* is
one of the ground Stones laid down for the Art, and
the breaking it is a nice Divifion of that *Meafure*,
and certainly muft anfwer more, the more you can
divide it. Upon the whole, it is of prodigious Advantage in both Swords. I have often broke a Head,
or hit my Opponent in other Parts, by judging the
proper *Diftance*, and breaking a trifling *Meafure*,
that is, by a fmall drawing back of my Head and
Contraction of my Body, I have efcaped his Blow, and
gone directly to his Head or Face without a *Parry:*
Here it is, in a manner, one Motion, and wants no
Comparifon of Time to the ftopping your Opponent's
Blow firft, and then making yours. So, in the
Small-Sword, it is of proportionable Ufe; and in

both

both, by being an exact Judge of your *Distance*,
you gain your *Time*; by which you will be able to
execute any thing you attempt. I believe there
have been few Hints given but will hold good in
either Sword, and sufficiently evince their near re-
lation. I will yet mention one thing more, which
is relative to both, and must recommend it for a
Point as profitable as any I have yet proposed in the
Art; and this is the stepping forwards in your *Parry*.
Let me be rightly understood,—The common Practice in Small and Back, is to retire in the one, from
your Adversary's *Thrust* while you *parry* it, and then
advance with your own; in the other, to step back
(which is much the same) in stopping his Blow, and
then come forward with your own. Here is your
manifest loss of Time, by which you are to compass
every thing, and without which you will not know
how, and why you do any thing. Alas! this giving way in your *Parade*, is no more nor less than
Fear of your Adversary's Arm and Distrust of your
own, which, till you can put a thorough Confidence
in, you never will be Master of your Sword. But
if you dare trust to your *Parade*, and so boldly rely
upon it, as to step in with it, in Small or Back, I
will engage that, if you *parry* your Man, he will
never get away from your Return. O! what a faving

ing of *Time* and ſhortning of *Meaſure* here is! for
by your *Longe* gained beforehand in your *Parade*,
inſtead of your Sword, you may lay your Finger
upon his Body. Let others recommend retiring as
much as they will, I am for advancing, or at leaſt
keeping your Ground ; but if you are weak in the
Practice, it is then neceſſary to retire for ſhelter. If
you give ground to your Adverſary, he will be very
forward to pour in his *Thruſts,* or *Blows* upon you ;
but if, upon his offering to advance, you ſtand firm
with your Foot and Arm in the Line, I will warrant
he will be more ſhy of approaching you. But then
how much more Danger muſt he be in, if you ſtep
with your right Leg and extend your Arm? By this
you will deprive him of his *Meaſure*, and have Opportunities of timing him in his advancing. This
Doctrine will hold good in both Small and Back-
Sword, and though they may differ in ſome trivial
Points, yet in the other fundamental Principles, eſſential to the Science, they mutually anſwer and
coincide.

Before I enter upon the Characters of the moſt
eminent Maſters, who have come within my Obſervation, I muſt take notice of the Superiority the
Back-Sword has over the Small, in point of Uſe. In-

deed

deed as we cannot put a Stop to the natural Paſſions
of Mankind, which, according to their Conſtitu-
tion and Temperament, more or leſs excite them to
Miſchief, if not proportionably checked by Reaſon;
we muſt endeavour at the readieſt Means of putting
it out of their Power to do us that Miſchief their
Paſſions prompt them to. It is therefore requi-
ſite to learn the Small-Sword, in order to guard
againſt the Attempts of that Man, with whoſe bru-
tal Ferocity no Reaſon will prevail: But then that
Neceſſity is productive of Pain and Miſery, though
it tends to the Preſervation of your Life. Killing
a Man, when you are forced upon the Defenſive,
clears you in human Laws; but how far you are
juſtified in Chriſtianity, the Goſpel beſt can tell you.
There is a Conſciouſneſs attends all Actions, which is
the ſtrongeſt Monitor; and that Conſciouſneſs will
not leave a Man undiſturbed after his Fellow-Crea-
ture is laid bleeding at his Feet, though from the
higheſt Provocation, and in his neceſſary ſelf-defence.
But Laws divine as well as human juſtify and pro-
tect you in your Country's Cauſe. Sure the wide
Difference between killing Numbers of your Enemy
in Battle, and one Man in a Quarrel, ever ſo much
in your own Defence, every calm thinking Man cannot but allow.

It

It is therefore that the Small-Sword, in point of true Reason, is not neceffary; it is only a fubfervient Inftrument to our Paffions. This is viewing it in the tendereft Light; but I fear it oftener proves, proportionably to it's Practice, an Incentive and Encouragement to Mifchief.

But the Back-Sword, fure, muft be diftinguifhed from the other, becaufe it is as neceffary in the Army, as the other is mifchievous in Quarrels, and deadly in Duels. The Small-Sword is the Call of Honour, the Back-Sword the Call of Duty. I wifh Honour had more Acquaintance with Honefty than it generally has. There is a Kind of Honour, which will carry a Man behind *Mountague* Houfe with another, when it will not pay his Debts, though he has wherewithal to do it. True Honour muft be very intimate with Honefty, and I will venture to affirm that, where the latter is not, the former has but a mean Exiftence. It need not be faid I here difcourage the Small-Sword, I only oppofe it's Abufe; I own, I have preached a little, but I think what I have advanced is true Doctrine: But as few of us can arrive to that prodigious Meeknefs, it is neceffary to be Mafters of our Sword, to guard againft thofe Paffions we cannot put a Stop to. I am not that
Saint

Saint to advife a Man to let another pull him by the
Nofe ; but then I would have him to be the brave
Ufer of his Sword, and not the quarrelfome. Quarrel-
fomenefs and Bravery, I take to be Strangers, and the
more Bravery I have found in a Man, I have always
obferved in him the more Unwillingnefs to quarrel.
I yet highly recommend the Small-Sword teaching,
if it were only (as I have before hinted) to introduce
you better, and eftablifh you ftronger in the Back-
Sword. The Back-Sword muft be allowed effen-
tially neceffary among the Horfe ; and I could wifh
it were more practifed, than I find it is. Sure it
ought to be a Part of a Trooper's Duty to learn the
Back-Sword, as much as of the Foot to learn the
common Exercife ; and the Exercife of the former's
Sword ought to be urged, as much as that of the
latter's Firelock. If a Troop of FIGS were engaged with a Troop of Men, ignorant of the Back-
Sword, I would afk, which has the better Chance? I
believe it will be granted, that a confiderable fuperior Strength in the latter would not be an
equivalent Advantage to the Skill and Judgement
of the former.

We are allowed to be more expert in the Back-
Sword than any other Nation, and it would be a
pity,

pity, if we were not to continue so. In FIG's
Time, the Spirit of it was greatly kept up; but I
have been often sorry to find it dwindle, and in a
Manner, die away with him. It must be allowed
that those amphitheatrical Practices were productive
of some ill, as they gave some Encouragement to
Idleness and Extravagance among the Vulgar. But
there is hardly any good useful Thing, but what
leaves an Opening for Mischief, and which is not liable
to Abuse. Those Practices are certainly highly necessary, and the Encouragement of Back-Sword
Fighting, and Boxing, I think commendable; the
former for the Uses which have been mentioned; the
latter, and both; to feed and keep up the British
Spirit. Courage I allow to be chiefly natural, pro-
bably owing to the Complexion and Constitution of
our Bodies, and flowing in the different Texture of
the Blood and Juices; but sure it is, in a great
measure, acquired by Use, and Familiarity with
Danger. Emulation and the Love of Glory are great
Breeders of it. To what Pitch of daring do we not
see them carry Men? And how observable is it in
Miniature among the Boys, who, almost as soon as
they can go alone, get into their Postures, and bear
their little bloody Noses, rather than be stigmatised
for Cowards?

CHARACTERS

CHARACTERS *of the* MASTERS.

TIMOTHY BUCK was a moſt ſolid Maſter, it was apparent in his Performances, even when grown decrepid, and his old Age could not hide his uncommon Judgement, He was the Pillar of the Art, and all his Followers, who excelled, built upon him.

Mr. MILLAR was the palpable Gentleman through the Prize-Fighter. He was a moſt beautiful Picture on the Stage, taking in all his Attitudes, and vaſtly engaging in his Demeanor. There was ſuch an eaſy Action in him, unconcerned Behaviour and agreeable Smile in the midſt of Fighting, that one could not help being prejudiced in his Favour.

FIG was the Atlas of the Sword, and may he remain the gladiating Statue! In him, Strength, Reſolution, and unparallel'd Judgement conſpired to form a matchleſs Maſter. There was a Majeſty ſhone in his Countenance, and blazed in all his Actions, beyond all I ever ſaw. His right Leg bold and firm, and his left which could hardly ever be diſturbed, gave him the ſurpriſing Advantage already proved, and ſtruck his Adverſary with Deſpair and Panic.

Panic. He had that peculiar way of ftepping in, I fpoke of, in a *Parry*; he knew his Arm and it's juft time of moving, put a firm Faith in that, and never let his Adverfary efcape his *Parry*. He was juft as much a greater MASTER, than any other I ever faw, as he was a greater Judge of *Time* and *Meafure*.

WILLIAM GILL was a Swords-Man formed by FIG's own Hand, and by his Example turned out a complete Piece of Work. I never beheld any Body better for the Leg than GILL. His Excellence lay in doing it from the *Infide*; and I hardly ever knew him attempt it from the *Outfide*. From the narrow Way he had of going down (which was moftly without receiving) he oftener hit the Leg than any one; and from the drawing Stroke, caufed by that fweeping Turn of the Wrift, and his proper way of holding his Sword, his Cuts were remarkably more fevere and deep. I never was an Eye-Witnefs to fuch a Cut in the Leg, as he gave one BUTLER, an *Irifhman*, a bold refolute Man, but an aukward Swords-Man. His Leg was laid quite open, his Calf falling down to his Ancle. It was foon ftitched up; but from the Ignorance of a Surgeon adapted to his mean Circumftances, it mortified: Mr. *Chefelden* was applied to for Amputation, but too

G   late

late for his true Judgment to interfere in. He immediately perceived the Mortification to forbid his Skill; and refufed to be concerned in what he knew to be beyond his Power. But another noted one was applied to, who, through lefs Judgment, or Value for his Character, cut off his Leg above the Knee, but the Mortification had got the Start of his Inftruments, and BUTLER foon expired.

JOHN PARKS of *Coventry* was a thorough Swords-Man, and an excellent Judge of all it's Parts. He was a convincing Proof of what I advanced about the natural Supplenefs in fome Men's Joints. No Man bid fairer for an acquired Spring than he; but notwithstanding the vaft Exercife, through fuch Numbers of Battles fought for twenty Years, he never could arrive to it. He ftill remained heavy, flow, and inactive, and had no Friend to help him, but his ftaunch Judgement.

SUTTON was a Contraft to the other. As PARKS had a clear Head upon a clumfy Body and ftiff Joints; fo SUTTON had a nimble Body and very agile Joints under a heavy Head. He was a refolute, pufhing, aukward Swords-Man; but by his bufy intruding Arm, and fcrambling Legs, there

were

were few Judgements but what were difordered and
difconcerted. FIG managed him the beft of any,
by his charming Diftinction of *Time* and *Meafure*,
in which he far excelled all, and fufficiently proved
thefe to be the Sword's true Foundation.

Mr. JOHNSON is a ftaunch Swords-Man. I do
not know any one now who has fo great a Share of
Skill and undaunted Refolution, mixed together.
He is a thorough MASTER of the true Principles of
the Back-Sword; but I muft take the Liberty to
fay, that his Joints are ftiff and flow in Action;
while I allow that his Judgement furprifingly makes
up that Defect. JOHNSON fights moft from the
Hanging, and executes more from it, than any I
ever faw from that unready Guard. I have often
thought it a great Pity a Man of his found Knowledge of the Sword, fhould have fo much recourfe
to the *Hanging*. I own the Word Recourfe fits not
JOHNSON, becaufe, as I faid before, it is a kind of
fheltering Guard, and in others moftly ufed to fhift
from Danger. I am fure that Fear pitches not his
Hanging; and he has as little occafion for a Shelter
from his Adverfary, as any Man I have known. He
fully proves it, as he differs from all the reft in ufing
that Guard. The others ufe it in a Retreat, he

advances

advances with it, and maintains it through the whole Battle with unshaken Firmness.

Mr. SHERLOCK must be pronounced an elegant Swords-Man, with uncommon Merit. His Designs are true and just, encouraged by an active Wrist and great Agility of Body. He pitches to the Small-Sword Posture, the Recommendation of which I here repeat. I know there are great Demurrs against it, but I will venture to justify him in it. He is certainly right to use that Guard, most properly called a Guard, which best stops the too near Approach of his Adversary, and at the same Time supplies him with more readiness to Action. But though I am willing to give every Man his due Merit, I cannot step into the Filth of Flattery; therefore must confess, Mr. SHERLOCK is not faultless. I will point out one Defect, and leave it to Judges whether I am right in my Observation. It is his Subjection and Proneness to starting, by which he evidently may put himself in the Power of a Man of much inferior Judgement. I have often seen Mr. SHERLOCK engaged with a Man of far less Abilities than himself, when, upon a bare Stamp with the other's Foot, and Movement of his Sword, he has hurried back with Precipitation. Sure Mr. SHERLOCK must own he hereby gives his Oppofer great Advantage; however, I leave him with this Acknowledgement, that if he had Mr. JOHNSON's firm ftable Refolution, he would rival any I have mentioned.

I conclude with JOHN DELFORCE, and though he never fought with the Sword, I think it would be unpardonable not to give him a Place among the beft of them; for fure none more fit, more able to bring up the Train. He is a very proper Cafe, or Cover to the whole Picture, and may ftand the guarding Centinel of the Art. I venture to proclaim him the only Rival to FIG's Memory. He is fo well known for a Cudgeller on the Stage, that I need not lofe any Time in reviving him to Thought. He is an in-contefted Pattern among Spectators, and has made every Body forely fenfible of his Abilities with the Stick, who dared difpute it with him. My Head, my Arm, and Leg are ftrong Witneffes of his con-vincing Arm. As I faid before, I have tried with them all, and muft confefs my Flefh, my Bones re-member him the beft. He ftrongly evinces with the Stick, what he would execute with the Sword. JOHN DELFORCE has every Ingredient to compound a per-fect Swords-Man, proper Strength, unerring Judge-ment, and fufficient Experience. He has a Spring

in

in the Wrift more ready and powerful than any I
have feen, and FIG feems to have bequeath'd to
him his Infight into *Time* and *Meafure.*

BOXING.

BOXING is a Combat, depending more on
Strength than the Sword: But Art will yet
bear down the Beam againft it. A lefs Degree of
Art will tell for more than a confiderably greater
Strength. Strength is certainly what the Boxer
ought to fet out with, but without Art he will fucceed but poorly. The Deficiency of Strength may
be greatly fupplied by Art; but the want of Art
will have but heavy and unwieldy Succour from
Strength.

Here it may not be amifs to make fome little
anatomical Enquiry into the advantageous Difpofi-
tion of the Mufcles by the juft Pofture of the Body,
and the acting Arm. I will venture to dabble a
little in it; but cry Mercy all the while. If I make
a Piece of Botch-Work of it, forgive the poor Anatomift through the Swords-Man.

The

The Strength of Man chiefly confifts on the Power of his Mufcles, and that Power is greatly to be in-creafed by Art. The Mufcles are as Springs and Levers, which execute the different Motions of our Body; but by Art a Man may give an additional Force to them.

The nearer a Man brings his Body to the Center of Gravity, the truer Line of Direction will his Mufcle act in, and confequently with more refifting Force. If a Man defigns to ftrike a hard Blow, let him fhut his Fift as firm as poffible; the Power of his Arm will then be confiderably greater, than if but flightly clofed, and the Velocity of his Blow vaftly augmented by it. The Mufcles which give this additional Force to the Arm, in fhutting the Fift, are the Flexors of the Fingers, and the Exten-fors are the oppofite Mufcles, as they open or ex-pand the fame; yet in ftriking, or ufing any violent Efforts with your Hand, thefe different Orders of the Mufcles contribute to the fame Action. Thus it will appear, that when you clofe the Fift of your left Arm, and clap your right Hand upon that Arm, you will plainly feel all the Mufcles of it to have a re-ciprocal Swelling. From hence it follows, that Mufcles, by Nature defigned for different Offices,

mutually

mutually depend on each other in great Efforts. This Confideration will be of much Advantage in that artificial Force in Fighting, which beats much fuperior Strength, where Art is wanting.

The Pofition of the Body is of the greateft Confequence in Fighting. The Center of Gravity ought to be well confidered, for by that the Weight of the Body being juftly fufpended, and the true Equilibrium thereby preferved, the Body ftands much the firmer againft oppofing Force. This depends upon the proper Diftance betwen the Legs, which is the firft Regard a *Boxer* ought to have, or all his manly Attempts will prove abortive. In order to form the true Pofition, the left Leg muft be prefented fome reafonable Diftance before the Right, which brings the left Side towards the Adverfary; this the right-handed Man ought to do, that, after having ftopped the Blow with his left Arm, which is a Kind of Buckler to him, he may have the more Readinefs and greater Power of ftepping in with his right Hand's returning Blow. In this Pofture he ought to referve an eafy Flexion in the left Knee, that his Advances and Retreats may be the quicker. By this proper Flexion, his Body is brought fo far forward, as to have a juft Inclination over the left Thigh, infomuch

much that his Face makes a perpendicular or straight Line with the left Knee; whilst the right Leg and Thigh in a slanting Line, strongly prop up the whole Body, as does a large Beam an old Wall. The Body by this means is supported against all violent Efforts, and the additional Strength acquired by this Equilibrium, is greatly to the Purpose. How much greater Weight must not your Adversary stand in need of, to beat you back from this forward inclining of the Body, than the so much less resisting Reclination of it? By this disposed Attitude you find the whole Body gently inclining forward with a slanting Direction, so that you shall find from the *Outside* of the right Ancle all the way to the Shoulder, a straight Line of Direction, somewhat inclining, or slanting upward, which Inclination is the strongest Position a Man can contrive; and it is such as we generally use in forcing Doors, resisting Strength, or pushing forward any Weight with Violence: For the Muscles of the left Side, which bend the Body gently forward, bring over the left Thigh the gravitating Part, which by this Contrivance augments the Force; whereas, if it was held erect or upright, an indifferent Blow on the Head, or Breast, would overset it. The Body by this Position has the Muscles of the right Side partly relaxed, and partly contracted, whilst

H   those

thofe of the Left are altogether in a State of Contraction; but the Referve made in the Mufcles of
the right Side, is as Springs and Levers to let fall
the Body at Difcretion.

By delivering up the Power to the Mufcles of the
left Side, which, in a very ftrong Contraction, brings
the Body forward, the Motion which is communi-
cated, is then fo ftrong, that, if the Hand at that
Time be firmly fhut, and the Blow at that Inftant
pufhed forward, with the contracting Mufcles, in
a ftraight Line with the moving Body, the Shock
given from the Stroke will be able to overcome a
Force, not thus artfully contrived, twenty times as
great.

From this it is evident, how it is in our Power
to give an additional Force and Strength to our
Bodies, whereby we may make ourfelves far fuperior
to Men of more Strength, not feconded by Art.

Let us now examine the moft hurtful Blows, and
fuch as contribute moft to the Battle. Though very
few of thofe, who fight, know, why a Blow on
fuch a Part has fuch Effects, yet by Experience
they know it has; and by thefe evident Effects,
they

they are directed to the proper Parts; as for In-
stance, hitting under the Ear, between the Eye-
brows, and about the Stomach. I look upon the
Blow under the Ear to be as dangerous as any, that
is, if it light between the Angle of the lower Jaw
and the Neck; because in this Part there are two
Kinds of Blood Veffels confiderably large; the one
brings the Blood immediately from the Heart to the
Head, whilft the other carries it mediately back.
If a Man receive a Blow on thefe Veffels, the Blood
proceeding from the Heart to the Head, is partly
forced back, whilft the other Part is pufhed forwards
vehemently to the Head : The fame happens in the
Blood returning from the Head to the Heart, for part
of it is precipitately forced into the latter, whilft the
other Part tumultuoufly rufhes to the Head; whereby the Blood Veffels are immediately overcharged,
and the Sinus's of the Brain fo overloaded and com-
preffed, that the Man at once lofes all Senfation,
and the Blood often runs from his Ears, Mouth and
Nofe, altogether owing to it's Quantity forced with
fuch Impetuofity into the fmaller Veffels, the Coats
whereof being too tender to refift fo great a Charge,
inftantly break, and caufe the Effufion of Blood
through thefe different Parts.

H 2

This

This · is not the only Confequence, but the Heart being overcharged with a Regurgitation of Blood (as I may fay with refpect to that forced back on the fucceeding Blood coming from it's left Ventricle) ftops it's Progrefs, whilft that Part of the Blood coming from the Head, is violently pufhed into it's right Auricle; fo that as the Heart labours under a violent Surcharge of Blood, there foon follows a Cardiaca or Suffocation, but which goes off as the Parts recover themfelves and pufh the Blood forward. The Blows given between the Eye-brows contribute greatly to the Victory: For this Part being contufed between two hard Bodies, *viz.* The *Fiſt*, and *Os frontale*, there enfues a violent Ecchymofis, or Extravafation of Blood, which falls immediately into the Eye-lids; and they being of a lax Texture incapable of refifting this Influx of Blood, fwell almoft inftantaneoufly; which violent Intumefcence foon obftructs the Sight. The Man thus indecently treated, and artfully hoodwinked, is beat about at his Adverfary's Difcretion.

The Blows on the Stomach are alfo very hurtful, as the Diaphragm and Lungs fhare in the Injury. The Vomitions produced by them I might account for, but I fhould run my anatomical Impertinences too far. I ·

I would here recommend to thofe who Box, that on the Day of Combat they charge not their Stomachs with much Aliment; for by obferving this Precaution, they will find great Service. It will help them to avoid that extraordinary Compreffion on the *Aorta Defcendens,* and in a great meafure preferve their Stomachs from the Blows, which they muft be the more expofed to, when diftended with Aliments. The Confequence of which may be attended with a Vomiting of Blood, caufed by the Eruption of fome Blood Veffels, from the overcharging of the Stomach: Whereas the empty Stomach, yielding to the Blow, is as much lefs affected by it, as it is more by it's Refiftance, when expanded with Food. Therefore I advife a Man to take a little Cordial Water upon an empty Stomach, which, I think, would be of great Service, by it's aftringing the Fibres, and contracting it into a fmaller Compafs.

The Injury the Diaphragm is fubject to from Blows, which light juft under the Breaft-Bone, is very confiderable; becaufe the Diaphragm is brought into a ftrong convulfive State, which produces great Pain, and leffens the Cavity of the Thorax, whereby the Lungs are in a great Meafure deprived of their Liberty, and the Quantity of Air retained in them,

from

from the Contraction of the Thorax through the convulsive State of the Diaphragm, is so forcibly pushed from them, that it causes a great Difficulty of Respiration, which cannot be overcome till the convulsive Motion of the Diaphragm ceases.

The artful Boxer may, in some Degree, render the Blows less hurtful on this Part, by drawing in the Belly, holding his Breath and bending his Thorax over his Navel, when the Stroke is coming.

I have mentioned Strength and Art as the two Ingredients of a Boxer. But there is another, which is vastly necessary; that is, what we call a Bottom. We need not explain what it is, as being a Term well understood. There are two Things required to make this Bottom, that is, Wind and Spirit, or Heart, or wherever you can fix the Residence of Courage. Wind may be greatly brought about by Exercise and Diet; but the Spirit is the first Equipment of a Boxer. Without this substantial Thing, both Art and Strength will avail a Man but little. This, with several other Points, will appear more fully in the Characters of the Boxers.

CHARACTERS

CHARACTERS *of the* BOXERS.

ADVANCE, brave BROUGHTON! Thee I pronounce Captain of the *Boxers.* As far as I can look back, I think, I ought to open the Characters with him: I know none fo fit, fo able to lead up the Van. This is giving him the living Preference to the reft; but, I hope, I have not given any Caufe to fay, that there has appeared, in any of my Characters, a partial Tincture. I have throughout confulted nothing, but my unbiafs'd Mind, and my Heart has known no Call but Merit. Wherever I have praifed, I have no Defire of pleafing; whereever decry'd, no Fear of offending. BROUGHTON, by his manly Merit, has bid the higheft, therefore has my Heart. I really think all will poll with me, who poll with the fame Principle. Sure there is fome ftanding Reafon for this Preference. What can be ftronger than to fay, that for feventeen or eighteen Years, he has fought every able *Boxer* that appeared againft him, and has never yet been beat? This being the Cafe, we may venture to conclude from it. But not to build alone on this, let us examine farther into his Merits. What is it that he wants? Has he not all that others want, and all the beft can have? Strength equal to what is hu-

man

man, Skill and Judgement equal to what can be acquired, undebauched Wind, and a bottom Spirit, never to pronounce the Word ENOUGH. He fights the Stick as well as moſt Men, and underſtands a good deal of the Small-Sword. This Practice has given him the Diſtinction of *Time* and *Meaſure* beyond the reſt. He ſtops as regularly as the Swords-Man, and carries his Blows truely in the Line; he ſteps not back, diſtruſting of himſelf to ſtop a Blow, and piddle in the Return, with an Arm unaided by his Body, producing but a kind of flyflap Blows; ſuch as the Paſtry-Cooks uſe to beat thoſe Inſects from their Tarts and Cheeſecakes. No— BROUGHTON ſteps bold and firmly in, bids a Welcome to the coming Blow; receives it with his guardian Arm; then with a general Summons of his ſwelling Muſcles, and his firm Body, ſeconding his Arm, and ſupplying it with all it's Weight, pours the Pile-driving Force upon his Man.

That I may not be thought particular in dwelling too long upon BROUGHTON, I leave him with this Aſſertion, that as he, I believe, will ſcarce truſt a Battle to a warning Age, I never ſhall think he is to be beaten, till I ſee him beat.

About

About the Time I firſt obſerved this promiſing Hero upon the Stage, his chief Competitors were PIPES and GRETTING. He beat them both (and I thought with Eaſe) as often as he fought them.

PIPES was the neateſt Boxer I remember. He put in his Blows about the Face (which he fought at moſt) with ſurpriſing Time and Judgement. He maintained his Battles for many Years by his extraordinary Skill, againſt Men of far ſuperior Strength. PIPES was but weakly made ; his Appearance beſpoke Activity, but his Hand, Arm, and Body were but ſmall. Though by that acquired Spring of his Arm he hit prodigious Blows ; and I really think, that at laſt, when he was beat out of his Championſhip, it was more owing to his Debauchery than the Merit of thoſe who beat him.

GRETTING was a ſtrong Antagoniſt to PIPES. They contended hard together for ſome Time, and were almoſt alternate Victors. GRETTING had the neareſt Way of going to the Stomach (which is what they call the Mark) of any Man I knew. He was a moſt artful Boxer, ſtronger made than PIPES, and dealt the ſtraighteſt Blows: But what made

I

PIPES a Match for him, was his rare Bottom Spirit, which would bear a deal of Beating, but this, in my Mind, GRETTING was not fufficiently furnifhed with; for after he was beat twice together by PIPES, *Hammerfmith* JACK, a meer Sloven of a Boxer, and every Body that fought him afterwards, beat him. I muft, notwithftanding, do that Juftice to GRETTING's Memory, as to own that his Debauchery very much contributed to fpoil a great *Boxer*; but yet I think he had not the Bottom of the other.

Much about this Time, there was one WHITA-KER; who fought the *Venetian* GONDELIER. He was a very ftrong Fellow, but a clumfy *Boxer.* He had two Qualifications, very much contributing to help him out. He was very extraordinary for his throwing, and contriving to pitch his weighty Body on the fallen Man. The other was, that he was a hardy Fellow, and would bear a deal of Beating. This was the Man pitched upon to fight the *Venetian.* I was at *Slaughter's* Coffee-Houfe when the Match was made, by a Gentleman of an advanced Station; he fent for FIG to procure a proper Man for him; he told him to take care of his Man, be-

caufe

caufe it was for a large Sum ; and the *Venetian* was a Man of extraordinary Strength, and famous for breaking the Jaw-bone in *Boxing*. FIG replied, in his rough Manner, I do not know, Mafter, but he may break one of his own Countrymen's Jawbones with his Fift ; but, I will bring him a Man, and he fhall not break his Jaw-bone with a Sledge Hammer in his Hand.

The Battle was fought at FIG's Amphitheatre, before a fplendid Company, the politeft Houfe of that kind I ever faw. While the GONDELIER was ftripping, my Heart yearned for my Countryman. His Arm took up all Obfervation ; it was furprifingly large, long, and mufcular. He pitched himfelf forward with his right Leg, and his Arm full extended, and, as WHITAKER approached, gave him a Blow on the Side of the Head, that knocked him quite off the Stage, which was remarkable for it's Height. WHITAKER's Misfortune in his Fall was then the Grandeur of the Company, on which account they fuffered no common People in, that ufually fit on the Ground and line the Stage round. It was then all clear, and WHITAKER had nothing to ftop him but the bottom. There

was

was a general foreign Huzza on the Side of the *Venetian*, pronouncing our Countryman's Downfal; but WHITAKER took no more Time than was required to get up again, when finding his Fault in standing out to the Length of the other's Arm, he, with a little Stoop, ran boldly in beyond the heavy Mallet, and with one *English* Peg in the Stomach (quite a new Thing to Foreigners) brought him on his Breech. The Blow carried too much of the *English* Rudeness for him to bear, and finding himself so unmannerly used, he scorned to have any more doings with his slovenly Fist.

So fine a House was too engaging to FIG, not to court another. He therefore stepped up, and told the Gentlemen that they might think he had picked out the best Man in *London* on this Occasion: But to convince them to the contrary, he said, that, if they would come that Day se'nnight, he would bring a Man who should beat this WHITAKER in ten Minutes, by fair hitting. This brought very near as great and fine a Company as the Week before. The Man was NATHANIEL PEARTREE, who knowing the other's Bottom, and his deadly way of Flinging, took a most judicious Method to

beat

beat him.——Let his Character come in here——He was a moſt admirable *Boxer*, and I do not know one he was not a Match for, before he loſt his Finger. He was famous, like PIPES, for fighting at the Face, but ſtronger in his Blows. He knew WHITA-KER's Hardineſs, and doubting of his being able to give him Beating enough, cunningly determined to fight at his Eyes. His Judgement carried in his Arm ſo well, that in about ſix Minutes both WHI-TAKER's Eyes were ſhut up ; when groping about a while for his Man, and finding him not, he wiſely gave out, with theſe odd Words—Damme—I am not beat, but what ſignifies my fighting when I cannot ſee my Man ?

We will now come to Times a little freſher, and of later Date.

GEORGE TAYLOR, known by the Name of GEORGE the BARBER, ſprang up ſurpriſingly. He has beat all the chief Boxers, but BROUGHTON. He, I think, injudiciouſly fought him one of the firſt, and was obliged very ſoon to give out. Doubtleſs it was a wrong Step in him to commence a Boxer, by fight-ing the ſtanding Champion : For GEORGE was not

then

then twenty, and BROUGHTON was in the Zenith
of his Age and Art. Since that he has greatly distinguished himself with others; but has never engaged BROUGHTON more. He is a strong able Boxer,
who with a Skill extraordinary, aided by his Knowledge of the Small and Back-Sword, and a remarkable Judgement in the Crofs-Buttock-Fall, may con-
test with any. But, please or displease, I am re-
solved to be ingenuous in my Characters. Therefore
I am of the Opinion, that he is not over-stocked
with that necessary Ingredient of a Boxer, called
a Bottom; and am apt to suspect, that Blows of
equal Strength with his, too much affect him and
disconcert his Conduct.

Before I leave him, let me do him this Justice to
say, that if he were unquestionable in his Bottom,
he would be a Match for any Man.

It will not be improper, after GEORGE the BAR-
BER, to introduce one BOSWELL, a Man, who wants
nothing but Courage to qualify him for a compleat
Boxer. He has a particular Blow with his left Hand
at the Jaw, which comes almost as hard as a little
Horse kicks. Praise be to his Power of Fighting, his
excellent Choice of *Time* and *Measure*, his superior
Judgement,

Judgement, difpatching forth his executing Arm!
But fye upon his daftard Heart, that marrs it all!
As I knew that Fellow's Abilities, and his worm-
dread Soul, I never faw him beat, but I wifhed him to
be beaten. Though I am charmed with the Idea of
his Power and Manner of Fighting, I am fick at the
Thoughts of his Nurfe-wanting Courage. Farewel to
him, with this fair Acknowledgement, that, if he had
a true *Englifh* Bottom (the beft fitting Epithet for a
Man of Spirit) he would carry all before him, and
be a Match for even BROUGHTON himfelf.

I will name two Men together, whom I take to
be the beft Bottom Men of the modern Boxers:
And they are SMALLWOOD, and GEORGE STEVEN-
SON, the Coachman. I faw the latter fight BROUGH-
TON, for forty Minutes. BROUGHTON I knew to be
ill at that Time; befides it was a hafty made Match,
and he had not that Regard for his Preparation, as
he afterwards found he fhould have had. But here
his true Bottom was proved, and his Conduct fhone.
They fought in one of the Fair-Booths at *Tottenham*
Court, railed at the End towards the Pit. After
about thirty-five Minutes, being both againft the
Rails, and fcrambling for a Fall, BROUGHTON got
                                                    fuch

such a Lock upon him as no Mathematician could
have devised a better. There he held him by this
artificial Lock, depriving him of all Power of ri-
sing or falling, till resting his Head for about three
or four Minutes on his Back, he found himself recovering. Then loosed the Hold, and on setting
to again, he hit the Coachman as hard a Blow as
any he had given him in the whole Battle; that he
could no longer stand, and his brave contending
Heart, though with Reluctance, was forced to yield.
The Coachman is a most beautiful Hitter; he put
in his Blows faster than BROUGHTON, but then
one of the latter's told for three of the former's.
Pity—so much Spirit should not inhabit a stronger
Body!

SMALLWOOD is thorough game, with Judgement
equal to any, and superior to most. I know nothing SMALLWOOD wants but Weight, to stand
against any Man; and I never knew him beaten
since his fighting DIMMOCK (which was in his Infancy of Boxing, and when he was a perfect Strip-
ling in Years) but by a Force so superior, that to
have resisted longer would not have been Courage
but Madness. If I were to chuse a Boxer for my

Money

Money, and could but purchafe him Strength equal to his Refolution, SMALLWOOD fhould be the Man.

JAMES I proclaim a moft charming Boxer. He is delicate in his Blows, and has a Wrift as delightful to thofe who fee him fight, as it is fickly to thofe who fight againft him. I acknowledge him to have the beft Spring of the Arm of all the modern Boxers; he is a compleat Mafter of the Art, and, as I do not know he wants a Bottom, I think it a great Pity he fhould be beat for want of Strength to ftand his Man.

I have now gone through the Characters of the moft noted Boxers, and finifhed my whole Work. As I could not praife all in every Article, I muft offend fome; but if I do not go to Bed till every Body is pleafed, my Head will ake as bad as Sir *Roger*'s. I declare that I have not had the leaft Thought of offending throughout the whole Treatife, and therefore this Declaration fhall be my quiet Draught.

Let me conclude with a general Call to the true Britifh Spirit, which, like pureft Gold, has no Allay.

K

lay. How readily would I encourage it, through the most threatening Dangers, or feverest Pains, or Pledge of Life itself! Let us imitate the glorious Example we enjoy, in the faving Offspring of our King, and blessed Guardian of our Country. Him let us follow with our keen Swords, and warm glowing Hearts, in Defence of our just Cause, and Preservation of *Britain*'s Honour.

F I N I S.

Printed in the USA
CPSIA information can be obtained
at www.ICGtesting.com
LVHW010420300923
759528LV00010B/1181